God Is Love Alone

God Is Love Alone

Brother Roger of Taizé

continuum
LONDON • NEW YORK

Continuum

The Tower Building	15 East 26th Street
11 York Road	New York
London SE1 7NX	NY 10010

www.continuumbooks.com

Original French version © Ateliers et Presses de Taizé, F–71250
Taizé-Communauté, France 2001
English translation © Ateliers et Presses de Taizé, F–71250
Taizé-Communauté, France 2003

First published by Continuum 2003

Reprinted 2004, 2005

British Library Cataloguing-in-Publication Data

A catalogue record for this book is available from the British Library.

ISBN 0–8264–7020–3 (PB)

Typeset by Fakenham Photosetting Ltd, Fakenham, Norfolk
Printed and bound by MPG Books Ltd, Bodmin, Cornwall

Contents

Are There Realities Which Make Life Beautiful?

A simple trusting

Are there realities which make life beautiful and of which it can be said that they bring a kind of fulfilment, an inner joy? Yes, there are. And one of these realities bears the name of trust.

Do we realize that what is best in each of us is built up through a simple trusting? This is something even a child can do.

But at every age people can be marked by suffering – being abandoned by others, seeing those they love die. And for many people today their future is so uncertain they lose all delight in life.

For all, the source of confident trust is in God. God is love and forgiveness, and dwells at the centre of each person's soul.

Trust does not make us forget the suffering of so many unfortunate people across the earth.

Their trials make us reflect on the question: How can we be people who, sustained by a life of communion in God, search with others for ways of making the earth a better place to live in?

Trust does not lead us to flee responsibilities, but rather to remain present in places where human societies are in turmoil. It enables us to keep going forward even in the face of failures. This trust makes us able to love with a selfless love.

Today many young people across the earth are trying to heal divisions in the human family. Their confident trust can make life beautiful around them. Are they aware that, so often, a hope shines out from them?

For some forty years now, my brothers and I have been astonished to see young people coming to Taizé in ever-greater numbers.

Seeing so many young faces on our hill, not only from Western and Eastern Europe, but also more and more from other continents, we realize that they come with vital questions, especially this one: How can I find a meaning for my life? Some of them ask: How is God calling me?

With those we welcome either in Taizé itself, or in the small communities in different parts of the world where a few of our brothers live among the poor, or during the meetings held in large cities, we want to look for ways of finding new vitality, of living Christ for others.

We want to be people who listen, never spiritual masters. People who listen to them so that they can express not only their limits and their wounds, but also discover their gifts. We especially want them to glimpse a life of communion with God, with Christ, with the Holy Spirit.

Trying to understand everything in another person

More often than ever before young people ask me, 'What is the most beautiful thing in your life?'

Without hesitating I reply, 'First of all the common prayer, and in it, the long periods of silence.'

Then, immediately after that, the most beautiful thing in my life is when I am talking with someone alone, to perceive the whole human being, marked by a tragedy or by being torn apart from within, and at the same time possessing the irreplaceable gifts through which the life of God in that person is able to bring everything to fulfilment.

It is essential to try and comprehend the whole person by means of a few words or attitudes rather than by lengthy attempts at explanation. It is not enough simply to share what assaults a person within. It is vital to search for that special gift of God, the axis of their whole existence. Once this gift (or gifts) has been brought to light, roads forward lie open.

No dwelling on the knots, failures and conflicting forces; thousands of reasons for them can always be found. Move on as quickly as possible to the essential – uncovering the unique gift, the talents entrusted to every human being intended not to lie buried but to be brought to full life in God.

The most beautiful thing in my life? I could go on for ever ... Those rare occasions when I suddenly find myself free to drop everything and go out; walking for hours and conversing in the streets of some great city; sharing a meal with guests around a table ...

Do you recognize the way of hope?

Are there realities in the Gospel that make life beautiful? Yes, there are. And one of these is hope. It enables us to go beyond discouragements and even rediscover a zest for life.

And where is its source? It lies in the audacity of a life of communion in God. But how is this communion possible? God loved us first.[1] God seeks us tirelessly, even if we are unaware of it.[2]

There is another Gospel reality that makes life beautiful – peace of heart. In human beings there can be impulses, which can sometimes even lead to violence. Three centuries after Christ, a Christian from Milan named Ambrose wrote, 'Begin the work of peace in yourself so that, once you are at peace yourself, you can bring peace to others.'[3] The peace of our heart makes life beautiful for those around us.

Trust, hope and peace of heart are rooted in a mysterious presence, the presence of Christ. By the Holy Spirit he is there in each person, like someone who is humble of heart. And his voice says softly, 'Do you recognize the way of hope that is open for you?'

5

Then how can we keep from saying to Christ, 'I would like to follow you for my entire lifetime, but do you know how weak I am?' Through the Gospel he replies, 'I am familiar with your trials and your poverty. To remain faithful your whole life long, you think you have nothing, or almost nothing. But you are filled. Filled by what? By the presence of the Holy Spirit. His compassion illuminates even the shadows of your soul.'[4]

I cannot forget an evening in the summer of 1942, when I was still on my own in Taizé. I was writing at a small table. It was wartime. I knew I was in danger because of the refugees I was sheltering in the house. Some of them were Jews. There was a serious threat that I would be arrested and taken away. Members of the civilian police force had repeatedly come to question me.

That evening, with fear in the pit of my stomach, a prayer of trust took hold of me. I said to God, 'Even if I lose my life, I know that you, the living God, will continue what has begun here, the creation of a community.'

For those who seek with steadfast hearts to surrender themselves to Christ and to give him their entire lives, there is a choice to be made: to let an unbounded gratefulness to God well up in us. It paves the way for the spirit of praise.

God wants happiness for us.[5] What means most to us is to go from one discovery to another, from beginning to new beginning. Consenting again and again to the trials that so often are part of human life. Looking for peace of heart in all things. And life becomes beautiful ... And life will be beautiful. And what we never dared to hope for arises.

> *Holy Spirit, inner Light, in the ploughed-up ground of our life you come to place a humble trust in you. Therefore we want to welcome you in all simplicity, as poor people of the Gospel.*

Mystery of a Presence

Christ united to every human being

If it were possible to fathom a heart, what would we find there? We would be surprised to discover that in the depths of the human condition there lies the longing for a presence, the silent desire for communion. And then we discover in the Gospel a response to this longing. Saint John expresses it with these words: 'The light that shines on every human being came into the world.'[6]

This light is the light of the risen Christ. Perhaps we are hardly aware of it, but he remains close to every person.

And who is he, this Christ Jesus of whom the Gospel speaks?

From before the beginning of the universe, from all eternity, Christ was in God.[7]

He came among human beings as a humble man. If Jesus had not lived among us, God would be far away, and even unattainable. But

8

in his life, Jesus allowed God to shine through as he is.[8] And today, risen from the dead, Christ lives in each one of us by the Holy Spirit.[9]

A luminous Gospel insight reappeared during the Second Vatican Council: 'Christ is united to every human being without exception ...'[10] For a long time it had remained buried under the dust of the ages. Later, Pope John Paul II would add: '... even if he or she is not aware of it.'[11]

Every year, during a private audience with Pope John Paul II, my desire is to gladden his heart by sharing with him a hope that he caused us to discover. I have told him how much his striking intuition – Christ is united to every human being, even if they are not aware of it – could open onto an unclouded understanding of faith on earth.

Multitudes of human beings do not know that Christ is united to them and are unaware of the way he looks at every life with love. They know nothing about God, not even God's name. And yet God remains in communion with everyone. In the same spirit, the Orthodox Christian theologian Olivier Clément helps us understand that the invisible God is 'like an inrush of light, of peace and love' for every human being.[12]

My brothers and I discovered a similar intuition in an aged Russian Orthodox bishop named Serafim who visited us in Taizé. One evening, speaking to the young people in the church, with great clarity in his voice, he said, 'Every human being is inhabited by the Holy Spirit.' He was a bit hard of hearing, and he said in a loud voice to the brother beside him, 'Have they really understood? Every human being is inhabited by the Holy Spirit.'

In the seventh century Saint Maximus the Confessor wrote, 'The Holy Spirit is absent from no human being.'[13] Some people have learnt from Scripture that the Holy Spirit dwells within them. Others do not know it yet, and some will never know it on this earth but will discover it in the life of eternity.

The Holy Spirit, support and comfort

If Christ were not risen and if he had not sent his Holy Spirit, he would not be present with all people. He would simply be one more remarkable person in the history of humanity and it would not be possible to converse with him. We would not dare to tell him, 'Christ Jesus, I rely on you at every moment. Even when I am unable to pray, you are my prayer.'

Before leaving them, Christ assured his disciples that he would send them the Holy Spirit as a support and a comfort.[14] As a result we can make this discovery: just as Christ was present with his disciples on earth, so he continues through the Holy Spirit to be present for us today.

More easily grasped for some, more hidden for others, his mysterious presence is always there. It is as if we could hear him say, 'Are you not aware that I am alongside you and, through the Holy Spirit, I live within you? I will never abandon you.'[15]

This mysterious presence is invisible to our eyes. For all of us, faith always remains a humble trust in Christ and the Holy Spirit.

Faith is a simple reality, both for the most uneducated person who cannot even read or write, as well as for the most cultivated one. The Russian writer Tolstoy recounts that one day, while taking a walk, he met a peasant and they had a conversation. The peasant said to Tolstoy, 'I live for God.' In four words he expressed the depths of his soul. And Tolstoy said to himself, 'I have so much knowledge and culture, and yet I am unable to speak like this peasant.'[16]

Trust in God is not conveyed by means of arguments which want to persuade at all costs, and as a result end up causing anxiety and even fear. It is first of all in the heart, in the depths of our being, that a Gospel call is received.

A gleam in the night

Dazzling visit of the love of God, the Holy Spirit flashes through each human being like a light in their night. By this mysterious presence, the Risen Christ supports us. He takes everything upon himself, even the trials so hard to bear. It can happen that wonder at such a love leads you to say:

'This Jesus, the Risen Christ, was in me and yet I felt nothing of his presence. So often I was looking elsewhere for him. As long as I continued to run away from the wellsprings he had placed in the hollow of my being, I might well go far, very far, but I kept getting lost on roads that led nowhere. There seemed no way to find a joy in God.

'Then the time came when I realized that Christ had never left me. I hardly dared speak to him, but he understood, and already he spoke to me. When the veil of worry was lifted, the trusting of faith came to illuminate even my own night.'

Sometimes I wonder why this trust in Christ who comes to illuminate our night is so essential to me. And I realize that this comes from a childhood experience.

During the weeks before Christmas, I used to spend a lot of time in front of a manger scene looking at the Virgin Mary and the newborn infant at her feet. Such a simple image marks one for life. It enables us to realize one day that, through Christ, God himself came to be with us.

On Christmas Eve, we would go to church. One year, when I was five or six years old, the ground of the mountain village we lived in was covered with snow. Since I was the youngest, my father took me by the hand. My mother, my elder brother and my seven sisters followed behind. In the clear sky my father showed me the shepherds' star that the wise men had seen.

13

These moments come to my mind when I hear the reading from the apostle Peter: 'Fix your eyes on Christ as on a star shining in the night, until the day begins to dawn and the sun rises in your hearts.'[17]

> *Christ of compassion, at the wellsprings of your Gospel we discover that, although there may be a portion of darkness within us, there is above all in each person your mysterious presence.*

Loved with Eternity's Love

God loves us before we love God

'Do you love me?'

This is the last question that Jesus, risen from the dead, asked Peter.[18]

Before Jesus was tortured on a cross, Peter had denied him three times and was dismayed by what he had done. After his resurrection, Christ appeared to Peter. He did not condemn him for his denial. Christ was filled with compassion. He had been a human being. During his earthly life, he too had walked along ways of darkness.

To Peter, Christ says just four words, 'Do you love me?'

And Peter replies, 'Lord, you know that I love you.'

Jesus repeats a second time, 'Do you love me?'

Again Peter answers, 'But you know that I love you.'

A third time, Jesus insists, 'Do you love me more than the others do?'

Peter is troubled. 'Lord, you know everything; you know that I love you.'

Today, we too can say to him, 'Christ, if you ask us as you asked Peter, "Do you love me?", we stammer our reply. "You know that I love you, Christ, perhaps not as I would like to, but I do love you."'

Christ never obliges anyone to love him but he loved us first.[19] He remains alongside us like a poor man. He is there even in the barren events or in the weak spots of our life. His love is a presence of eternity.

God loves us before we love God – even a child is able to understand this Gospel reality. One day in the church, a child of nine came to say goodbye to me. He was leaving after having spent a week in Taizé. He loved taking part in our community prayer. He was going through the trial of being abandoned by someone dear to him – his father had left the family. I wrote down these words for him: 'God loved you before you love him; he has deep trust in you.' These words are a bit difficult for a child. Perhaps his grandmother will explain them to him. Perhaps he will understand them himself, since his trial developed a precocious maturity in him.

God loves us before we love God. I think I understood this when I was still a child, when as a family we read the story of Port-Royal-des-Champs.

Some summer afternoons we would get together to read texts aloud. Among the stories that were often read were some excerpts of the history of Port-Royal, written by Sainte-Beuve. It told of a Cistercian community of women that lived near Paris in the seventeenth century.

When the abbess died in 1602, Angélique Arnauld, the daughter of a Parisian lawyer, replaced her. According to the custom of the time, her grandfather had taken steps to ensure that she would be elevated to that office despite her young age. She remained in the monastery against her wishes and lived there for several years in great inner distress.

One day, writes Sainte-Beuve, when the young abbess was seventeen years old, a priest passed through and gave a meditation to the community. It was common knowledge that this priest led a disordered life, but that day he expressed clearly God's love, his inexhaustible and unlimited goodness. The priest's words caused an inner upheaval in the young

Angélique Arnauld. 'God touched me so deeply that, from that moment on, I considered myself more fortunate to be a religious than I had previously thought myself unfortunate to be one.'

As a result, returning to the wellsprings of their vocation, she introduced radical changes in the life of the community; gradually it became known far and wide and had a great impact on people's lives. Among others, Blaise Pascal's sister entered the community. Men came to live beside the monastery for shorter or longer periods of prayer and study; they were known as the 'Messieurs de Port-Royal.'

My mother had so much admiration for that period of the history of Port-Royal-des-Champs that she placed a portrait of Mother Angélique Arnauld on her desk. 'She's my invisible friend,' she used to say. And myself, I was captivated to discover what a few women, living in community, had been able to accomplish.

Close to our house there was a large yew tree with very dense foliage. One day when I was about sixteen, I stopped by that tree and said to myself, 'If those few women, responding in all lucidity to a call to community life and giving their life for Christ, had so much impact on those around them, could not a few men living in community do the same thing?'

Since then, I think that I never lost the intuition that community life could be a sign that God is love, and love alone. Gradually the conviction took hold that it was essential to create a community with men determined to give their whole life and who would always try to understand one another and be reconciled, a community where kindness of heart and simplicity would be at the centre of everything.

His love is a fire

God loves us before we love God. Loved with eternity's love, we sense that our response is above all to surrender ourselves.

And so, our soul is filled with a thirst – to surrender everything to God. 'And our heart keeps on longing until it rests in God.'[20]

Every human being yearns to love and be loved. But the question remains: why are some people aware that they are loved while others are not?

When we are listened to, wounds from a recent or distant past find relief. This can be the beginning of a healing of the soul.

Listen to what makes others feel bad about themselves. Try to understand what lies beneath their hearts. And little by little, even in a ground ploughed up by trials, God's hope can be sensed, or, at least, a fine human hope.

It happens that, when we accompany another person, the one who listens is led to the essential himself, although the other may be unaware of it.

Listen and keep on listening – someone who makes use of their intuition throughout their lifetime becomes able to understand almost without words those who come with something to confide. Listening in this way can contribute to a very broad vision of human beings, inhabited by both fragility and radiance, by fullness and the void.

Some years ago I met with a young priest from Italy every day for a week. In him I saw at close hand Christ's holiness in a human being. At times I could not say anything except, 'Dare to weep!' Once I even took a handkerchief from my pocket for him. Weep, because it is not possible to bear alone, in stony silence, the struggle he had to wage. Face to face with him, I could touch on what it can mean for a person to be abandoned. I saw that there exist people of silence who radiate communion.

As the days went by, the face of Christ appeared in that man so harrowed by his struggles. The depth of his gaze could conceal nothing of his successive ordeals. He brought me into the heart of one of the greatest mysteries – the gift of one's entire existence for love.

Before parting, after so many days of closeness, I knelt for him to give me his blessing.

Do not quench the fire

Another encounter with a priest remains branded in my heart. Two of my brothers and I spent one Christmas Eve in a women's prison in Santiago de Chile. After Midnight Mass we shared a meal with some of the prisoners. Some were sentenced under common law but there were also political prisoners. Almost all were in tears. Some faces were ravaged, others trans-figured with serenity.

The priest told us, 'These are not bad women. Some may be a little bit questionable. I know them. I have been coming here every day for twenty years.'

Looking at that priest's face and learning of his faithful daily visits, a question filled my heart and I asked him, 'Where does it come from, this passion of yours for God and for communion between people? Did you have a grandmother or mother who prayed for you?'

'Yes,' he replied, 'my mother. When I left her in our little village in Spain twenty-two years ago, she came to the door with me and said a few words, the last I ever heard her say. "Be a good priest, my son." I never saw her again. A year later she died.' There are mothers who leave an indelible mark in the life of their sons and remain an immutable support.

That Christmas Eve, we had come to visit some prisoners. We also found a vocation in the fullest sense of the word, a human life in which the absolute could be read, lived for the sake of Christ and the Gospel.

Above all by the gift of our lives, God desires that both fire and Spirit be made perceptible in us.

Yes, his love is a fire. However poor we may be, let us not quench the fire, let us not quench the Spirit.[21]

And the humble trusting of faith is communicated like fire spreading from one person to the next.

> *God of all mercy, you found no other way*
> *to express to human beings that you are*
> *love, and love alone, so through Christ you*
> *came to earth as a humble person. And so,*
> *happy are we for loving Christ without*
> *having seen him!*

A Breath of Trusting

Choosing to love

Like an almond tree that blossoms at the first hint of spring, a breath of trusting makes the deserts of the heart burst into flower again.

Borne forward by this breath, who would not wish to alleviate human suffering and trials? Even when our feet stumble along a stony path, who would not wish to put these Gospel words into practice in their life, 'Whatever you do for the least, the most destitute, you are doing for me, Christ'?[22]

A century after Christ, a believer wrote, 'Clothe yourself in cheerfulness ... Cleanse your heart of harmful sadness and you will live for God.'[23]

Whoever lives for God chooses to love. Making such a choice one's own calls for unfailing vigilance. A heart determined to love can radiate goodness without end. Its greatest concern is to relieve the torments of others nearby and far away.

All who live for God sense that their entire existence is staked on the trust they place in Christ and in the Holy Spirit. If an inner fog were to make us drift away from the trusting of faith, Christ does not abandon us for all that. No one is excluded either from his love or from his forgiveness.[24] And if discouragement and even doubts arise within us, Christ does not love us any the less. He is there, shedding light on our path. And his call rings out, 'Come, follow me!'[25]

How often, during a private conversation with a young person, do I hear these questions, 'How can I be myself? How can I fulfil myself?' Some people are preoccupied by this to the point of anguish. Then I think of what one of my brothers once said. 'Christ does not say to me, "Be yourself." He says, "Be with me." Christ does not tell us, "Find yourself." He says, "You, follow me!"'

Does not the Holy Spirit enable us to leave a 'harmful sadness' behind by casting worry, anguish and fear into the crucible of prayer?

But so often we do not know how to pray! But then 'the Holy Spirit comes to help us in our weakness.'[26] The Spirit inspires and sustains our prayer more than we realize, recreating an inner unity when we are scattered or fragmented within. It is so true that there is no inner unity without peace of heart.

During his earthly life, Jesus prayed and his face was transfigured by light. But he also prayed with tears of supplication.[27]

Singing to Christ until we are joyful and serene

Following Christ with a steadfast heart does not mean lighting fireworks that flare up brightly and then go out. It means setting out, and then remaining, on a road of trust that can last our whole life. This trust always remains humble. If faith became a spiritual pretension it would lead nowhere.

A breath of trusting can be held back by tormenting memories of a recent or distant past. The Gospel encourages us not to look back,[28] not to linger over our failures.

Endless discussions with ourselves can clutter our being and keep peace of heart far away. At such times it takes courage to say to Christ,

'Inner Light, do not let my darkness speak to me!'[29]

Gospel joy, the spirit of praise, will always involve an inner decision.

Daring to sing to Christ until we are joyful and serene ...[30] Not with just any kind of joy, but with that joy which comes straight from the wellsprings of the Gospel.

Some people discover the depths of joy in consenting to the fact that one day they shall leave behind life on earth for a life that will have no end. As for me, I know that there is peace of heart in realizing that death is not the end; it opens the way towards a life where God welcomes us to himself forever. Naturally I will be sorry to leave my brothers, to leave so many young and not-so-young people whose intuitions have been beacons of light in my life. I will be sorry to leave Marie, the four month-old infant whom Mother Teresa placed in my arms so that I could take her from Calcutta to Taizé in order for her precarious health to be cared for.

But through the Gospel we understand that God wants happiness for us and that we cannot add a single day to our lives by worrying about it.

When my mother was already very elderly, she had a heart attack. As soon as she could speak again she uttered these words, 'I am not afraid of dying; I know in whom I believe ... but I love life.' And on the day she died she whispered, 'Life is beautiful ...' She wanted to give comfort and hope to someone close to her who could not bear seeing her depart. Consenting to our own death allows us to rediscover a flow of life.

One day, for a meal to celebrate a brother's birthday we invited Cristobal, a young man from the south of Spain. We talked about the flooding in Andalusia. He recalled how, in Malaga, when he was ten, he saw a torrent of water and mud come crashing down. Before his very eyes, the house of his best friend Eduardo was destroyed. As the walls collapsed he saw Eduardo's body being swept away by the waters.

During the whole of the following week, every day he spent time in the local church before the Eucharistic reserve. He wrestled within himself, in the presence of God, asking why Eduardo was gone. After eight days he found peace and could trust once more. He had said to God, 'You are all I have.'

At that point in his story, Cristobal began to cry; he wept for a long, long time. We decided to leave the dessert for the next meal and Cristobal promised, 'I will come and sing flamencos.' At table that evening, tirelessly, Cristobal sang.

A road that leads to the holiness of Christ

With a heart that trusts, in the presence of God's infinite compassion, our innermost being can sometimes be seized and becomes able to glimpse a road that leads to the holiness of Christ. So many people radiate holiness without being aware of it, and perhaps without even daring to believe it.

The human family will know a peaceful trust as long as there are men, women and children who love, pray and dare to take risks for Christ and the Gospel.

During a visit to New York, in the house where we were staying the cook was an old Brazilian woman. I had learned her story. After an operation for cancer, she said, 'It is better that I am the one to have this illness, because I know how to suffer.'

As we parted, I came to her with the words, 'I want to kiss the hands of a saint.'

'Don't say that,' she replied. 'Call me a missionary.'

To which I answered, 'A saint is a witness to Jesus Christ and you are that more than many others.' Her brow was dark, almost black, marked by cobalt treatment. But her face was radiant.

If our steps were to become heavy and sluggish, would we still be able to discern the desert flower? It blossoms at sunrise, in the hours of constant new beginnings, when a gentle breeze of trusting enables us to go a long way on the road of a serene goodness.

And this trust can enable us both to love life on earth and at the same time to long for a beyond, for a life that will never end.[31]

> *Holy Spirit, mysterious presence, you open for us that Gospel reality which consists in loving with a selfless love. And you enable us to understand that what matters most is not to lose the spirit of mercy.*

A Healing of the Heart

Christ never threatened anyone

Saint John's Gospel assures us that Christ did not come to earth to condemn the world but so that, through him, every human being might be saved, reconciled.[32]

And yet it can happen that the human heart is inhabited by a secret fear of God. Where does this guilt feeling come from, sometimes found already in little children? To think that God condemns human beings is one of the greatest obstacles to faith.

If only those called to speak about the Gospel or to pray aloud could say to themselves, 'May your prayer or your words never contain the slightest threat in the name of God!' God does not make use of fear to impose himself upon human beings. Christ did not threaten anyone, even when he was mistreated.[33]

In my family, when we were children, my mother was never severe. She never scolded us.

She would speak to us; she explained things. I can never remember seeing her lose her temper. She used to say about people who got angry, 'I think they are losing their mind.'

If we only knew to what extent some children need to be looked at with trust so that they can rediscover joy at being alive. In a child's heart, the knowledge that he or she is tenderly loved, and also forgiven, can be a source of peace for an entire lifetime.

It is so essential for children to be understood and not hurt by those to whom they are entrusted. If only parents or teachers would never use the authority given by age to be less than kind to a child.

Living lives of forgiveness

God is never, never at all, a tormentor of the human conscience. He buries our past in the heart of Christ and is going to take care of our future.

If we had to love God for fear of punishment, that would not be love. God weaves our life, like a beautiful garment, with the threads of his forgiveness. The certainty of God's forgiveness is one of the most generous realities of the Gospel.[34] It brings freedom – freedom beyond compare.

The contemplation of his forgiveness becomes a radiant kindness in a simple heart that lets itself be led by the Spirit.

Why dwell on what hurts, both in yourself and in others? You know the words of one of the first witnesses to Christ, 'Even if our hearts condemn us, God is greater than our hearts.'[35]

Christ never invites you to be preoccupied with yourself, but rather to a humble repentance of heart. What does that mean? It is that movement of trust whereby you cast your faults on him. And then you are released, ready to live the present moment intensely, never discouraged because always forgiven.

Those who root their lives in forgiveness are able to pass through rock-hard situations like the water of a stream which makes its way in early springtime through the still-frozen ground.

Forgiveness can change our heart: severity and harsh judgments recede and leave room for an infinite goodness. And we become capable of seeking to understand more than to be understood.

In December 1976, a young Lebanese man by the name of Gassibeh was returning from Beirut, where he was studying, to spend Christmas in his village. At that time Lebanon was in the throes of war, and the young man was killed in an ambush on the road. He had had a presentiment of what was going to happen and he left a letter to his family in his room at the university. He wrote, 'I see myself being killed on the road leading to my village. If that happens, I say to my mother and my sisters: do not be sad; we shall meet again. Forgive those who killed me. May my blood, mingled with the blood of all the victims who have fallen, from all sides and from all religious traditions, be offered as the price of the peace, love and mutual under-standing which have disappeared from this country. Pray, pray, and love your enemies.'

Six years later, two of my brothers and I were spending Christmas in Lebanon, on the eve of our European young adult meeting in Rome. War was still being waged in that beloved country. We went to visit Gassibeh's mother.

In the poor hovel where his mother was staying after being forced to leave her village, she accomplished within herself what her son had asked for: she had forgiven. She bore on her face the mark of those who have gone as far as possible on that road, the road of forgiving even those who were responsible for the tragedy. Nothing is less natural for the human heart than to pray for one's enemies.

Before we took our leave, in front of a large photo of her son, Gassibeh's mother and her youngest daughter sang to Christ who remained alongside her in the depths of her misfortune. Then, in a sign of blessing, she raised her hands to make the sign of the cross over us.

The transfiguration of our being goes forward step by step

Even if, at times, we seem to be in the night, a light is shining in the midst of the darkness. The apostle Peter invites us to focus our eyes on that light 'until day begins to dawn and the sun rises in our hearts.'[36]

A plant not turned towards the light withers away. If believers were to linger in the shadows, could trust grow within their hearts?

The Gospel comes to turn our lives upside down: by the Holy Spirit, Christ penetrates what worries us about ourselves. He reaches what seems to be out of reach, so that even the darkest places can be illuminated by his presence.

When the night becomes dark, his love is a fire.[37] It causes what had been smouldering under the ashes to burst into flame. Christians like Saint John of the Cross and Saint Theresa of Avila began a new life of faith fairly late in life. They spoke of the fire that was often kindled with all the thorns of their past.

Marie Noël, a twentieth-century French poet of profound faith, wrote, along the same lines, 'The best and most nourishing souls are made of a few great and radiant acts of goodness and a thousand tiny obscure miseries which feed their goodness, like the wheat that lives from the decomposition of the soil.'[38]

One evening, during a prayer in a cathedral in Belgium full of young people, one of them asked me, 'Brother Roger, show us the way to God!'

I replied, 'I don't know if I can show the way to God. But, in my old age, I can share a personal experience that has marked my entire life.

'When I was young I was an invalid for many years, the result of tuberculosis followed by a serious relapse. I had time to read, to meditate, and to discover God's call – a vocation that could last for a lifetime.

'When death seemed close, I sensed that, even more than the body, it is the depths of the self that are in need of healing. And our hearts are healed above all by a humble trust in God.

'Those years of illness allowed me to realize that the source of happiness is not in prestigious talents or great expertise, but in the humble giving of oneself – yes, the quite humble giving of oneself – in order to understand others with kind-heartedness.'

Little by little, I realized that creative energies could arise even from a childhood or an adolescence that had been humiliated. The apostle Paul expresses this Gospel reality with great intuition when he writes, 'It is when I am weak that I am made strong in God.'[39]

We would never wish a child or a youth to lose hope because he or she has been humiliated. But in cases when people have experienced deep trials linked to humiliations in their early years, it turns out that Christ's compassion was always present.

And Christ can bring out of these trials a great boldness to create in God, to run the risks of faith. He passes through our limits, failures and inner nights. He transforms them, he transfigures them throughout our lifetime.

An imperceptible inner change, the transfiguration of our being goes forward step by step. It is the beginning of a life that will know no end, already here on this earth.

When we are racked by the awareness of our limits or feelings of inferiority, we are surprised to find that Christ enables us to set out again with new energy.

The elderly Pope John XXIII passed through times of trial and used to say, 'I am like a bird singing in a thorn bush.'[40] We too would like to communicate joy despite the thorns that prick us. Not just any kind of joy, but the joy which consists in knowing that Christ loves every human being as if he or she were the only one.[41]

God enables us to be born and reborn in him when we welcome his trust and his forgiveness into our lives. If we let ourselves be clothed in forgiveness as in a garment, we will glimpse a light shining in our night.

*Jesus our hope, even when you were
mistreated and abused, you did not
threaten; you forgave. In seeking to follow
you, we too would like to be able to forgive
and forgive again.*

All God Can Do Is Give His Love

God shares the sufferings of each person

There are physical forms of violence on earth, such as war, torture, murder ... There are other more subtle forms of violence that are concealed in cunning tactics, suspicion, mistrust, humiliation, an unkept promise ...

And there are all those children, all those young people, wounded by broken relationships, to such an extent that some of them ask: does my life still have any meaning? In the presence of physical or moral violence in the human family, a question plagues us: if God is love, where does evil come from?

No one can explain the why of evil. The philosopher Paul Ricoeur writes, 'I have nothing to reply to those who say, "There is too much evil in the world for me to believe in God." God's only power is unarmed love. God does not want us to suffer. From being all-powerful, God becomes "all-loving". God has no other power than to love and, when we are suffering, to address a word of assistance to us. Our difficulty is to be able to hear it.'[42]

Six centuries after Christ, a Christian thinker, Saint Isaac of Nineveh, taking up the words of Saint John, 'God is love',[43] concluded, 'All God can do is give his love.'[44]

God is never an indifferent witness to human affliction. God suffers with the innocent victims of incomprehensible trials; God suffers with each person. There is a pain that God experiences, a suffering felt by Christ. In the Gospel, Christ expresses his solidarity with human suffering, weeping at the death of someone he loved.[45]

Did not Christ come to earth so that every human being could know that he or she is loved?[46]

And so the heart can awaken to the wonder of a love.

Suffering does not come from God

Two of my brothers and I were in Ethiopia one day, during the Advent season. At Christmas we visited a village of lepers. A woman named Adjebush told us her story. When she found out she had leprosy, her husband left her. Her four sons were fighting in the war; one had been killed, and she had no news of the others. Her little girl was sleeping beside her. Her deepest desire was that her daughter would understand the faith. With both legs amputated, Adjebush could not even go out to beg.

Then she spoke these unexpected words, 'I weep inner tears and sometimes outer tears, but I know that Christ is here, standing beside me.' And she began to praise God by lifting up her hands, according to the Coptic Orthodox tradition.

We asked ourselves: where does she get such trust? We realized that she drew it from the wellsprings of prayer. She had let a whole inner life develop within her; she had gone forward in a life of deep communion with God. Adjebush understood that suffering does not come from God. She knew that God was not the author of her misfortunes and trials.

As she kept on praying, she began to comment on our visit to her, and her words turned into a kind of hymn on her lips. She said to God, 'It's Christmas and they came to see me; it's Christmas and they did not stay home, they came here.'

We were astonished to realize that often we perceive a unique, luminous Gospel insight in people who are totally destitute. All of us would like to be as close to God as that humble Ethiopian Orthodox woman. And all of us, like her, would like to discover in the simplicity of our hearts that Christ is present, close to us.[47]

Alleviating human suffering

In this period of history, there is an impressive awakening of the Christian conscience with regard to human suffering.

Everywhere in the world, there are Christians who are giving their lives. They are trying to be present amidst the increasingly rapid evolutions of society. Some take on responsibilities that are often very specific. They try to show a way forward to those who are paralyzed by fear of the future, or tempted to withdraw in an attitude of 'everyone for himself'.

These Christians are not satisfied by an economic growth that benefits only part of the population. They are also attentive to the situation of some people who today have the mysterious face of the 'suffering servant' described in the Bible: humiliated, ill-treated, with nothing to attract us, they bear our diseases.[48]

From the very beginnings of Taizé, it was clear that we were going to do all in our power to live Christ for others and to alleviate human suffering.

During the First World War, while the bombs were falling, my mother's mother had sheltered refugees in her home north of Paris. Her example inspired me when, in 1940, I left Switzerland to go to live in France, where my mother came from, in order to create a community. War had broken out once again and I was convinced I had to offer help to people who were undergoing trials.

I settled in a house in the village of Taizé which I was able to purchase for a very low price, the cost of a good car. As the last of nine children I had few material resources. I could not count on my father to help me, since it was to be expected that he would first of all assist the older ones to get a start in life. I was able to buy the house thanks to a modest loan.

After having fixed up the house a bit, I quickly made contact with some friends in Lyons, among them Roland de Pury. The north of France was occupied. Roland de Pury told me about people who were trying to reach the south of the country and suggested that I offer hospitality to some of them, who needed a place to hide for a few days or even longer. Some of them were Jews.

Since I was still alone, I asked the youngest of my seven sisters, Genevieve, to come and help me. She was the only one who was not married. Material resources were limited. There was no running water; we had to go to the village well to get water to drink. At that time you needed ration cards to buy food, and it was impossible to get any for the refugees. So we had very little to eat, mainly soups made of grilled corn flour that we bought cheaply at the nearby mill.

We only asked the refugees their first names, since it was risky for them to have their background known. Out of discretion towards them, I used to pray alone. I often went to sing in the woods away from the house. Genevieve explained to the refugees who were Christians that it was better to pray alone, so that those who were Jewish or unbelievers would not be made to feel ill at ease by prayers together.

During the summer of 1942, we received an important visit. One of our two cousins, Pierre Marsauche, was in the army. His words made us realize that everything was getting more and more serious in Europe, that large numbers of people were in danger of death. His younger brother Jacques also came, and the time we spent together was a real comfort.

Knowing that my sister and I were exposed, my parents had asked a friend of theirs, a retired French army officer, to keep an eye on us. He did so conscientiously. In October 1942, he warned us that we had been found out, that not only did we have to stop sheltering refugees, but also to leave Taizé for a time.

Slightly less than two years later, in the autumn of 1944, I was able to return. This time I was not alone; we were four brothers.

In 1945, a young man from the region started an association to take care of children who had lost their families because of the war. He asked us to welcome a number of them in Taizé. A community of men could not take care of children. So I telephoned my sister Genevieve and asked her to come back for a time; the children needed a mother. An artist with all her being, she had undertaken advanced studies on the piano. She did not hesitate to answer yes, however. And gradually she realized that she could not leave those children, that she had to devote her life to them. At the beginning there were three of them; the months passed, and soon there were twenty or so. She set up home with them in an old house in the village.

Five of the twenty boys were from Soviet Georgia; their father had been forced to flee his country. When they arrived in France, they were placed in a refugee camp. Their father fell seriously ill. An Orthodox Christian, he had admirably prepared his two eldest sons for his death. After he died, the five boys came to live in Taizé with my sister.

Her whole life long, she lived in the same old house with other children as well, until they were grown up. They still come to stay with her today, bringing their own children and grand-children. Later she welcomed Marie, the four month-old baby that Mother Teresa entrusted to my care, and who grew up in Genevieve's home.

Seeing the faithfulness of my sister Genevieve over the years, I have understood that it is kind-heartedness above all that has enabled her to weather so many events. Kind-heartedness is an invaluable stimulus to action.

> *Holy Spirit, Comforter, in a world where we can be disconcerted by the suffering of the innocent, enable us to be for them a reflection of your compassion.*

The Hope of a Communion

Living as people who are reconciled

As we enter the third millennium are we sufficiently aware that, two thousand years ago, Christ came to earth not to start a new religion but to offer every human being a communion in God?[49] Ever since he rose from the dead, Christ's presence has been made tangible through a communion of love which is the Church.[50]

Will Christians have hearts large enough, imaginations open enough, love burning enough to discover this Gospel way: to live without delay as people who are reconciled?[51]

Although the ecumenical vocation has fostered remarkable dialogues and sharing, how can we forget these words of Christ, 'Go first and be reconciled'?[52] By putting off the reconciliation of Christians to a later date, ecumenism could keep alive illusory expectations without realizing it.

When Christians remain in great simplicity and in an infinite goodness of heart, when they seek to discover the profound beauty of the human soul, they are led to be in communion with one another in Christ.[53]

Credibility can be reborn for the younger generation when that communion which is the Church becomes transparent by striving with its whole soul to love and to forgive, when, even with a minimum of resources, it becomes welcoming, close to human suffering. Never distant, never on the defensive, freed from all forms of severity, it can let the humble trusting of faith shine right into our human hearts.

'Christianity is just beginning,' writes the Orthodox theologian Olivier Clement. 'We are witnessing the appearance of a Christianity that is poor and free, able to testify to the Gospel in a simpler and more straightforward way.'[54]

Yes, Christ calls us, the poor of the Gospel, to live out the hope of a communion. This is something even the very simplest can achieve.[55]

Some questions have been preoccupying my brothers and myself for many years now: why do so many young people, in vast regions of the world, take part less and less in prayer in churches, or even not at all? Why do some say that they are bored when they attend a service of worship?

If Christ was not being deserted in this way in the communion of his Body, his Church, if there was not such an absence of young people in the churches, our community would not have been stimulated to welcome the young so that they could pray, share and be listened to. And to welcome them not just in Taizé, but also during meetings in Europe or in different continents, including in places where some of our brothers share the life of the poor.

In Taizé or during these meetings, we have discovered that the beauty of a community prayer sung together can allow young people to let the desire for God well up in them, and also to enter into the depths of contemplative waiting.

A Bible scholar, Stanislas Lyonnet, attempted to formulate in a few words a way of communion accessible to the young. He said, 'Every baptized person who disposes him or herself inwardly to place their trust in the Mystery of the Faith belongs to the Church.'

During his visit to Taizé in 1986, Pope John Paul II awakened in our community an awareness that sustains our vocation with the young. The pope told us in particular, 'By desiring to be yourselves a parable of community, you will help all whom you meet to be faithful to their church affiliation, but also to enter more and more deeply into the mystery of communion that the Church is in God's plan.'[56] Words like these prepare a road for people who are searching with all their soul to live in communion.

Can I recall here that my maternal grand-mother discovered intuitively a sort of key to the ecumenical vocation, and that she opened for me a way to put it into practice? Marked by the witness of her life, while I was still very young, following her I found my own Christian identity by reconciling within myself the faith of my origins with the mystery of the Catholic faith, without breaking fellowship with anyone.

'Concentric circles that are larger and larger'

In the middle of the twentieth century there appeared a man by the name of John, born to a humble peasant family in the north of Italy. In 1959, when he announced a council, that aged man, John XXIII, pronounced some words that were among the most crystal-clear possible. They are able to make that communion of love that is called the Church totally transparent. Here are these words of light, 'We do not want to put history on trial. We will not try to determine who was wrong or who was right; both sides bear responsibility. We will only say: let us be reconciled!'[57]

John XXIII had the intuition that a council could open ways for Christians to live in communion. We were filled with gratefulness when we realized that he wished us to be present at the Council as observers. I remember the day when the letter arrived: to be invited to take part in that search was a gift from God!

The Second Vatican Council began in 1962. With clear words, John XXIII was able to find expressions that encouraged people to go forward, without losing any time listening to prophets of doom. The day the Council opened he said, 'In the current situation of society, the only thing these prophets of doom see is ruin and calamity; they say that things have become much worse in our day, as if everything were perfect before; they announce catastrophes, as if the world were close to its end.'[58]

Another thing he said that same day is astonishing because of its intuitive power and remains relevant today. 'The Church prefers to make use of the medicine of mercy rather than to wield the weapons of severity.'[59]

One day, in a private audience, John XXIII confided to us how he sometimes took decisions while praying. 'I speak with God,' he said. There was a moment of silence, and he added, 'Oh! Quite humbly, oh! Quite simply.'

After a meeting we had with him on 13 October 1962, we learned that he had said about us, 'We did not negotiate; we spoke together. We did not argue; we loved each other.'

Our last meeting took place on 25 February 1963. There were three of us – I was with my brothers, Max and Alain. Suffering from an advanced stage of cancer, at the age of eighty-two, the Holy Father knew his death was approaching and we had been warned of this. We were told that our audience would be fixed for a day when John XXIII was not in pain, a day when he would be rested and we would be his only visitors. That audience lasted an unusually long time. Aware that we would never see him again, we wanted to hear a kind of spiritual testament from his lips. John XXIII was concerned that we not be worried about the future of our community. Making circular gestures again and again with his hands, he emphasized, 'The Catholic Church is made up of concentric circles that are larger and larger, always larger.'

During that last meeting with him, we saw tears in his eyes because, he told us, some of his intentions had recently been deliberately misinterpreted.

When I learned of his death on 3 June 1963, my brothers and I were on our way to evening prayer. And from the depths of my being this question arose: what would become of our community without John XXIII?

After the pope's death, twice we welcomed to Taizé his youngest brother, Giuseppe Roncalli, with some members of his family. That elderly man observed everything attentively. He noticed among other things how rudimentary the accommodation for young people on our hill was.

One evening he said to his grandson Fulgenzio, 'It was my brother the pope who began what will come out of Taizé.' That peasant from Bergamo had realized to what extent we loved his brother and that the love was reciprocated.

'The divisions between Christians need to be healed'

During the summer of 1992, we received a visit that gladdened our hearts: the Archbishop of Canterbury, George Carey, primate of the Anglican Communion, came to Taizé with a thousand young Anglicans from different countries. They spent a week with the other young people who were there.

As soon as he arrived, the archbishop spoke words that clearly showed what his heart was like: 'First I thought I would go to Taizé to give a teaching to the young Anglicans. Then I said to myself that it was more important to go as they do, as a pilgrim. The divisions between Christians are a burden that I bear; they need to be healed. I believe in reconciliation with the

Catholic Church and I would like to see it happen in my lifetime.'

As I watched him leave at the end of the week, I said to myself, we have discovered in him a man who wants to understand contemporary situations, and to do so with great simplicity of heart. That makes him so authentic. He is one of those of whom it can be said: for anyone who knows how to love because of Christ, life is filled with serene joy.

Two years later, in April 1994, the fourteen bishops of the Lutheran Church of Sweden came to our community for several days of prayer and reflection. It was the first time that all the bishops of the Church of Sweden went abroad together.

We searched for answers with those men of open and generous heart to the question: how is it that, in vast regions of the earth, attentiveness to Christ is vanishing and many young people seem to be 'elsewhere'? Some of them once loved that communion which is the Church, but they lost interest when they did not immediately find a response to their longing there.

And we concluded with this question: how can the Church open the gates of compassion and kind-heartedness? It is so true that she is called to be first and foremost a reflection of Christ's compassion in the human family.

'Let God wipe away the evil past'

At the same period as John XXIII, in Istanbul, there was a man of the same prophetic vein, the Orthodox Patriarch Athenagoras.

In 1970, Brother Max and I had the opportunity of spending four days with him. What raised our hopes was the awareness that that this eighty-six year-old man – with so few means at his disposal and enmeshed in a complex political situation – could have an enormous impact both close at hand and far away. He had the greatness of the truly generous.

He had not been spared trials. He had understood the things that had to be changed in God's people, but the situation around him was such that he had to keep the best of his intuitions to himself. In spite of everything he remained hopeful. 'When I enter my bedroom in the evening,' he told us, 'I leave my worries at the door and I say: we'll see tomorrow!'

One day during a meal, the patriarch said to us, 'I would like you to take an icon from the cathedral home with you!'

I answered that we never accept gifts or presents for our community.

Then one of his collaborators chimed in, 'We have a cupboard full of icons in very bad shape; take one of those!'

We found one in the bottom of the cupboard. In the train on the way home it was disintegrating; bits of wood were crumbling into dust. It was so damaged that we had to have it restored three times. We still have it today. Set in a corner of my room, it supports the desire to pray, not with many words but with the heart.

Until the day I die, I will see the patriarch as he was when we took our leave. Standing in the doorway, he lifted his hands as if he were offering the chalice at the Eucharist and repeated once again, 'The cup and the breaking of the bread, there is no other way; remember ...'

The memory of an earlier visit with Brother Max is also etched in my mind. The patriarch wanted us to make a pilgrimage with him by car around Istanbul. Every time the car came to a place where a Christian had been martyred, he made his driver slow down or stop. We made the sign of the cross and we continued on our way.

That man of God had written, 'The evil past, full of separations and violence, remains alive in us and feeds fear and hatred. That is why we have to let God wipe away the evil past.'[60]

Another witness of the Orthodox Church has an important place in our community's memory. In 1962 Metropolitan Nikodim of St Petersburg came to spend two days with us. During a long sung prayer, he blessed the icon of the Virgin Mary that is venerated by many in the church of Taizé.

We saw him again in 1963 during the thousand-year celebrations of Mount Athos. Later, in June 1978, we visited him in St Petersburg, at that time still called Leningrad. How can we forget the nighttime train journey we took to get there? In those northern latitudes, the summer night was illuminated by a soft glow. We passed by farms with their wells topped by a long arm with which to draw water. People began working at dawn.

As we entered the seminary, Metropolitan Nikodim was in a chapel celebrating the ordination of a priest and a deacon. He was singing in his deep bass voice. Though he was still young, he had already had five heart attacks.

During our stay, a priest brought us from one church to another to pray. The Russian Christians who were praying there were animated by a boundless ardour. With deep prostrations they came and went from one icon to another. We discovered the supplication of a contemplative people. It was the eve of Pentecost. The metropolitan asked me to speak to the seminarians, then in the evening at his cathedral. In the grim period the Russian people were then going through, it was surprising to see so many young faces praying.

A few months later, in September 1978, despite his illness, the metropolitan went to Rome for the beginning of the ministry of Pope John Paul I. We were there also. After the celebration, the delegations present came one after another to be received by the new pope. While waiting, we exchanged a few words with the metropolitan and he told us he would soon return to Taizé. He was then taken into the pope's presence, there was a commotion, and we were told he had died in the pope's arms of a sixth heart attack. His body was placed in a small chapel, and Brother Max and I spent time praying there.

The metropolitan carried the hope of a communion in his heart. By his life he showed that the secret of the Orthodox soul lay above all in a prayer open to contemplation.

There is a question that is more urgent today than ever before: will Christians of the West and those of the East discover a deep trust in one another? Many Western Christians love their Eastern brothers and sisters because they have gone through numerous trials and in them are found gifts of communion that are so transparent.

For my part, this deep love for the Orthodox Church goes back to my childhood. During the First World War, Russians had to flee their land. They were Orthodox Christians. My mother received some of them in our home and I listened to their conversations; afterwards, she told me about the misfortunes they had undergone. When I was a bit older, we lived close to a Russian Orthodox church. We went there to take part in the prayer, to listen to the beautiful chants, and I tried to see in the people's faces the suffering of those Christians who had come from Russia.

Today, we try to be very attentive to the young people from Russia, Belarus, Ukraine, Romania, Serbia and Bulgaria who have been coming to Taizé in great numbers in the past few years. So many Orthodox Christians have known how to love and forgive in the midst of their trials. Goodness of heart is a vital reality for many of them. They are living witnesses to a trust in the Holy Spirit. By their focus on the resurrection, they strengthen us in the essential of the faith.

> *Jesus our peace, your Holy Spirit always opens a way forward for us, the way of abandoning ourselves in God. And we understand that loving means living a communion, with God and with those who are entrusted to us.*

From Doubt to Humble Trusting

Light will shine in the nights of the soul

We are in a world where light and darkness co-exist.[61]

As we aspire to the light, could doubt take hold of us? A Russian believer, Dostoyevsky, far from worrying about this, wrote, 'I am a child of doubt and unbelief. What terrible suffering it has cost me and still costs me, this longing to believe, which is so much the stronger in my soul as more arguments against it rise up within me ... My "hosanna" has passed through the crucible of doubt.'[62]

And yet Dostoyevsky could continue, 'There is nothing more beautiful, more profound, more perfect than Christ. Not only *is* there nothing, but there *can be* nothing.'[63]

When that man of God suggests that the non-believer co-exists in him with the believer, his

passionate love for Christ still remains undimin-
ished.

Happy are those who walk from doubt
towards the brightness of a humble trusting in
Christ! Just like the sun dispelling the morning
mist, light will shine in the nights of the soul.
Not an illusory trust but a clear-headed one, that
impels us to act in the midst of real-life
situations, to understand, to love.

Years ago, some of my brothers and I spent
some time in Calcutta, in a district of great
poverty. In the afternoons, Mother Teresa
would sometimes ask me to go with her to the
homes for the dying to visit lepers who were
simply there waiting for death. And every
morning, with one of my brothers who is a
doctor, we went to take care of children who
were seriously ill. It was a life-changing
experience. Sometimes children even died in our
arms.

From the very first day I took care of a little
girl of four months; her mother had died shortly
after she was born. They told me it was likely
that she would not live very long. Mother Teresa
put her in my arms and entreated me to take her
with me to Taizé so that she could receive

proper care. And I said to myself: if that child were to sense the anxiety I feel for her life, what would become of her?

And I continued: let your anxiety be transformed into the trust of faith. As long as the child lives, entrust her to God. Resting on your heart, she will at least have experienced the happiness of trust in her short life.

When we arrived in Taizé, the brothers gathered in my room to see the child. I placed the little girl, named Marie, on my bed and, for the first time, she began to gurgle like a happy baby.

And in the end she lived. She grew up in my sister Genevieve's home. Today she is an adult. She is my goddaughter and I love her like a father.

'Seek and you shall find'

It can happen that God seems to become distant. Some people are disconcerted by the impression that God is silent. Could the trusting of faith consist in saying 'yes' to God's love even if there is this deep silence within us?[64] Faith is like a surge of trusting repeated a thousand times over in the course of our life.

We need to remember that it is not our faith that creates God, and it is not our doubts that can cast him into nothingness. Even were we to feel no apparent resonance, the mysterious presence of Christ never disappears.[65] Although we may have the impression of an absence, there is above all the wonder of his continual presence.

When worries succeed in distancing us from the trusting of faith, some people ask themselves: have I become a non-believer? No, they are gaps of unbelief, nothing more.

The Gospel invites us to place our trust in Christ again and yet again, and to find in him a life of contemplation.[66] And Christ speaks these Gospel words to each of us, 'Seek, seek and you will find.'[67]

Happy are those who walk from doubt towards humble trusting! When my mother was already very elderly, one day she spoke to me about her own mother and said, 'You may not know that your grandmother, whom we loved and admired so much, did not find it easy to believe.'

'I did know it,' I replied, 'and I love her all the more for it.'

My grandmother went through great trials. Her three brothers died of tuberculosis, and her father also. Then later on, one of her sons died. She used to write notes in her Bible. I found there this prayer to God: 'I am not made for struggles ... I have doubts ... Help me!' And then these words, 'Lord, we are unable to wage this struggle, but that is a reason for not leaving you, for remaining close to you.'

For my part, I can say that when I was young, at a certain moment, my faith seemed to be shaken. I did not really call into question the existence of God. What I doubted was the possibility of living in communion with him. I wanted to be so honest that there were times when I no longer dared to pray. I thought that I needed to know God in order to pray.

One fine day, when I was still young, I opened an old book and my eyes fell on some lines written in archaic French. The author wrote that although God was not communicable, Christ made him known. 'Christ is the resplendence of God.' I never forgot that. It is Christ who enables us to understand that God loves us.[68]

In the summer of 1937 Lily, one of my seven sisters, the one to whom I had dictated my childhood poems and to whom I was very attached, fell seriously ill. She was the mother of five children. I realized that she was expected to die. Then I was able to say a prayer, these words of a psalm, 'My heart says of you: seek his face. I am seeking your face, O God.'[69] Those words seemed honest to me. I was able to kneel down and say that prayer. I realized that faith was in me and that it could be nothing other than a quite humble trust in God.

Surrendering ourselves to Christ

Even if our faith is very weak, can we realize that God has a call for each of us? What call? The Gospel enables us to understand that there is no greater love than to go to the extreme of self-giving.[70]

When God calls a person to a vocation for an entire lifetime, some are surprised to find themselves praying, 'Holy Spirit, you are the guardian of a lifelong vocation; give me what I need not to stop along the way.'

And if a doubt were to come welling up again? That does not mean that the desire for God has vanished. Four centuries after Christ, a believer named Augustine wrote, 'If you desire to see God, you already have faith.'[71]

The simple desire to welcome God's presence places a flame within us. Could that flame be only a pale glimmer? It already enables us to keep going through long nights in almost total darkness.

When we are assailed by gloom, boredom and disenchantment, there is a choice to be made. It consists in entrusting everything to the Holy Spirit again and yet again. And hope can spring to life once more.

One of the first brothers in our community is a support without being aware of it. For years now there have been times when he says, 'I rejoice in every instant that I live.' Like every human being, he has known trials. How can he rejoice in every instant? He knows what it means to hold firm and remain faithful in a vocation as the years pass. To keep going forward, he often prays by repeating these few words, 'Jesus, my joy, my hope and my life.'

In the face of the absolute claims of the Gospel, you may be taken aback. A believer of the first hour already said to Christ, 'I believe.'

But he immediately added, 'Help my unbelief.'[72]

Know once and for all that neither doubts nor the impression that God is silent can take his Holy Spirit away from you. What God asks of you is to welcome his love and to surrender yourself to Christ with a simple trust.[73]

> *God of all loving, you love and search for each of us even before we loved you. And we are seized with wonder to discover that you look upon every human being with infinite tenderness and deep compassion.*

Three Letters to Young People

A prospect of happiness?

If we could realize that a life of happiness is possible, even in hours of darkness . . .[74]

What makes life happy is to head towards simplicity – simplicity of our heart, and of our life.

For a life to be beautiful, extraordinary abilities or great expertise are not required. There is happiness in the humble giving of oneself.

When simplicity is closely linked to kind-heartedness, then even people without resources can create a space of hope around themselves.

Yes, God wants happiness for us! But he never invites us to remain passive, or indifferent to the suffering of others. On the contrary, God encourages us to be creators, and to manage to create even in times of trial.

Our life is not subject to the whims of fate or to a blind destiny. Far from it! Our life finds meaning when it is, above all, the living response to a call from God. But how can we recognize such a call and discover what God wants from us? God wants us to be a reflection of his presence, bearers of a Gospel hope.

All who respond to this call remain aware of their own frailties, and so keep these words of Christ in their heart: 'Do not be afraid; simply give your trust!'[75]

There are people who perceive, however faintly at first, that God's call for them is a vocation for their entire lifetime.

The Holy Spirit has the strength to sustain a 'yes' for our whole lives. Has he not placed in us a desire for eternity and the infinite?

In the Spirit, at every age, it is possible to find new vitality and to say to ourselves, 'Be steadfast of heart, and keep going forward!'[76]

And then, by his mysterious presence, the Holy Spirit brings about a change in our hearts, rapidly for some, imperceptibly for others. What had been obscure or even disturbing starts to become clear.

Until the end of our days, a 'yes' spoken in trust can bring so much clarity and joy.

Although we are called to make the gift of ourselves, we are not really built for such a gift. Christ understands our inner resistances. By overcoming them, we demonstrate our love to him.

Attentive to God's call, we understand that the Gospel invites us to take on responsibilities to alleviate human suffering.

The faces of the innocent, of a great many poor people across the earth, question us: how can we share a hope with those who are so deprived of it?

And Christ's words in the Gospel offer a crystal-clear reply, 'Whatever you do for the lowliest, you are doing for me.'[77]

All God can do is give his love, and suffering never comes from God. God is not the author of evil; he wants neither human distress, nor wars, nor natural disasters, nor violent accidents. God shares the pain of all who are undergoing times of trial and enables us to comfort those who are suffering.

God wants happiness for us: but where is the source of such a hope? It lies in a communion with God, alive at the centre of each person's soul.

Can we understand what we will be given? The day will come when the mystery of this communion with God takes hold of us. It touches what is unique and most intimate in the depths of our being.

God is Spirit[78] and his presence remains invisible. He lives within us always, in times of darkness as well as when everything is bathed in light.

Could there be chasms of the unknown in us, and also an abyss of guilt that comes from who knows where? God never threatens anyone,[79] and the forgiveness with which he inundates our lives brings healing to our soul.

How could a God of love impose himself by threats? Could God be a tyrant?

If doubts assail us, they are sometimes only interludes of unbelief, nothing more. Keeping watch over our thoughts can help us stand firm amidst the distractions that pull us in all directions.

Could the impression arise that God is far from me, as if for a fleeting moment the inward eye could no longer see? We should remember that God never withdraws his presence.

The Holy Spirit never leaves our soul: even at death communion with God remains. Knowing that God welcomes us forever into his love becomes a source of peaceful trust.

Our prayer is a simple reality. Is it perhaps no more than a poor sigh? God hears us all the same. We should never forget that, at the heart of every person, the Holy Spirit is praying.[80]

And remaining in silence in the presence of God is in itself an inner attitude which opens the way to contemplation.

A prospect of happiness? Yes, God wants happiness for us! And there is happiness in the humble gift of oneself.

Love and say it with your life*

*'Love and say it with your life'. These words were written three centuries after Christ by a Christian from North Africa, Saint Augustine.

Today more than ever before, a call is arising to

open paths of trust even in humanity's darkest hours. Can we hear that call?

There are people who, by giving themselves, attest that human beings are not doomed to hopelessness. Are we among them?

More and more people throughout the world are becoming aware of how urgent it is to come to the aid of the victims of poverty, a poverty that is constantly on the rise. This is a basic necessity to make peace on earth possible.

The disparity between the accumulation of wealth by some and the poverty of countless others is one of the most serious questions of our time. Will we do all in our power for the world economy to provide solutions?

Neither misfortunes nor the injustice of poverty come from God; all God can do is give his love.

And so we are filled with astonishment when we discover that God looks at every human being with infinite tenderness and deep compassion.

When we realize that God loves us, that God loves even the most forsaken human being, then our hearts open to others. We are made more aware of the dignity of the human person and we ask ourselves: how can we prepare ways of trust on earth?

However powerless we may be, are we not called to communicate a mystery of hope to those around us by the lives we live?

Others can recognize our trust in God when we express it by the simple giving of our own lives. Faith becomes credible and is passed on above all when it is lived out.

God's presence is a breath that fills the entire universe; it is an inrush of love, light and peace on earth.

Borne forward by this breath of life, we are drawn to live in communion with others and we are led to make the hope of peace a reality in the human family. May this communion and this hope shine out all around us!

By his Holy Spirit, God penetrates the depths of our being; he knows how we are longing to respond to the call of his love. And so we can ask him, 'How can I discover what you want of me? My heart is troubled: how can I perceive your call?'

And in inner silence this answer can well up:

'Dare to give your life for others; there you will find meaning for your existence.'

One day we may find ourselves saying to God:

'The days passed and I did not respond to your call. I went so far as to ask myself: do I really need God? Hesitations and doubts made me drift away from you.

'But even when I remained far from you, you were waiting for me. I thought I had been abandoned, and you were alongside me.

'Day by day, you renew within me the spontaneity which allows me to hold true in a "yes" to Christ. You look at me with such understanding that my "yes" will be able to carry me onward until my last breath.'

To remain faithful our whole lives long requires unflagging attentiveness.

In the course of our lifetimes the Holy Spirit comes to visit our inner nights, and gradually our whole being is transfigured.

In a world where new technologies are making possible advances never before imagined, it is important not to neglect fundamental values of the inner life – compassion, simplicity of heart and simplicity of life, humble trust in God, serene joy ...

The Gospel awakens us to compassion and to a kind-heartedness without bounds. There is nothing naive about this; it can require vigilance. And these values lead to discovery: seeking to make others happy liberates us from ourselves.

Looking at others with love allows the beauty of the human soul to reveal itself to us.

Simplicity of heart and life keeps us away from twisting paths where we risk going astray.

The most striking thing about the Gospel is forgiveness – the forgiveness that God gives us, and the forgiveness God asks us to give one another. Even when he was abused and mistreated, Jesus the Christ did not threaten anyone; he forgave.[81] Alive in God, he continues to offer the freedom of forgiveness.

There is no will to punish in God.

By forgiving us, God removes what has wounded our hearts, in some cases since childhood or adolescence.

Entrust all to God, even our worries ... And then we realize that we are loved, comforted, healed.

In the Gospel, Christ never calls us to sadness or gloom. On the contrary, he places peaceful joy within our reach, and even jubilation in the Holy Spirit.[82]

A young African who recently spent a year in Taizé explained how he gradually came to discover joy in the wake of great misfortune. When he was seven years old, his father was killed. And his mother had to flee far away. He said, 'I wanted to find my parents' love again, the love I had not known since childhood. So I sought an inner joy, hoping it would give me strength in the midst of suffering. It enabled me to leave behind the loneliness of my childhood. I realized how important joy is in order to change everyday relationships and to find inner peace.'[83]

God has breathed a soul into every human being.[84] That soul is invisible, just as God is invisible. It is there that our desire for a communion with God is born.

And how can we make this communion a reality? It is possible to encounter God truly in prayer, whether it is expressed with words or in silence.

Nothing brings us as close to God as prayer with others, when it is supported by the beauty of song.

Realizing that even death does not put an end to a communion with God brings peace to our hearts. Instead of leading to nothingness, it opens the way to a life of eternity when God welcomes our soul forever.

Even when there are doubts in us, the presence of the Holy Spirit remains, in days of peace as well as in times of dryness.

Are we not the poor of the Gospel? Our humble faith is enough to welcome God's presence. And the mere desire for it brings our soul back to life, on earth as in eternity.

A God who simply loves*

*'All God can do is love'. This conviction was expressed by a Christian thinker of the seventh century, Saint Isaac of Nineveh. He reached this conclusion after studying Saint John's Gospel for many years and meditating on the words 'God is love' (1 John 4:8).

All across the world, many among the younger generations are searching and asking themselves: is there any hope for our future? How can we go from worry to confident trust?

Our societies are sometimes shaken to their foundations. There is the uncertain future of humanity, with poverty constantly on the rise. There is the suffering of so many children, and all the broken relationships that leave hearts wounded.

And yet, even in the world's most troubled situations, do we not see on the horizon signs of an undeniable hope?

In order to go forward, it is good to know this: the Gospel offers such a shining hope that it can bring joy to our soul.

This hope is a path of light that opens up in our depths. Without it, all delight in living could vanish.

Where is the source of this hope? It is in God, a God who simply loves and can do nothing else, a God who never stops seeking us.

Our hope is renewed when we entrust ourselves humbly to God.

There is a force which dwells within us and

which is the same for everyone. This force is called the Holy Spirit, and whispers in our hearts, 'Surrender yourself to God in all simplicity; the little faith you have is enough.'

But who is this Holy Spirit? He is the one Christ Jesus promised in his Gospel when he said, 'I will never abandon you. I will always be with you through the Holy Spirit, who will support and comfort you.'[85]

Even when we think we are alone, the Holy Spirit is with us. His presence is invisible, yet it never leaves us.

And gradually we realize that the most important thing in life is to love with trust.

Trust is one of the humblest and simplest realities that exist, and at the same time one of the most basic.

When we love with trust we bring happiness to people around us, and we remain in communion with those who have gone before us and who are waiting for us in God's eternity.

When times of doubt arise in some people's lives, we should keep in mind that doubt and trust, like shadow and light, can co-exist within us.[86]

Above all let us remember these reassuring words of Christ, 'Do not be afraid or let your heart be troubled.'[87]

Then it becomes clear that faith is not the result of effort, but is a gift from God. It is God who enables us day after day to leave our hesitations behind and move towards trust in him.

All God can do is love, and his compassion is a source of life. May the day come when we can say, 'God of mercy, even if we had the faith to move mountains, without your love what would we be?[88] Yes, your love for each one of us remains forever.'

One of the clearest expressions of God's love is forgiveness. When we forgive in our turn, little by little our life changes.

Finding in forgiveness a breath of joy, we see all forms of severity towards others fade away; it is essential for harsh words and deeds to be replaced by boundless kindness.

Even before the time of Christ, a believer expressed this call, 'Leave your sadness behind; let God lead you to joy.'[89]

This joy heals the secret wound of the soul. It lies in the transparency of peaceful love, and needs our whole being in order to burst forth.

Very many people today aspire to live in a time of trust and of hope.

In human beings there can be impulses towards violence. For trust to arise on earth we need to begin within ourselves, making our way forward with a reconciled heart, living in peace with those around us.

Peace on earth is prepared insofar as we dare to ask ourselves: am I ready to seek inner peace and to go forward in selflessness? Even if I have very little, can I be a ferment of trust in my own situation, understanding others more and more?

As we remain before God in quiet waiting, will we open ways of peacemaking wherever oppositions arise?

When young people make a resolution for peace in their own life, they become bearers of a shining hope whose light radiates ever further outward.

At this time in history, the Gospel invites us to love and to say it by our existence. Faith becomes credible to those around us above all by the lives we lead.

This is also true for the mystery of communion that is the Body of Christ, his Church. A credibility that has often been lost can be reborn when the Church lives in trust, forgiveness and compassion, and when it welcomes with joy and simplicity. It then succeeds in communicating a living hope.

When our personal prayer seems poor and our words awkward, we should not let this bring us to a standstill.

Is not one of the deepest desires of our soul to live in communion with God?

Three centuries after Christ, an African believer by the name of Augustine wrote, 'A desire that calls out to God is already a prayer. If you want to pray ceaselessly, then never stop desiring . . .'

Great simplicity of heart sustains contemplative prayer. Simplicity is a source of joy. It enables us to surrender ourselves to God, to allow ourselves to be led to him.

In this life of communion, God, who remains invisible, does not necessarily communicate with us by means of human words. God speaks above all by silent intuitions.

Silence in prayer seems like nothing. And yet, in this silence the Holy Spirit can enable us to welcome God's joy – a joy which reaches down to touch the very depths of our soul.

In simple prayer, many people understand one day that God is calling them. What is God's call?

God wants us to prepare ourselves to be bearers of joy and peace.

Will we listen to God when his words ring out in us: 'Don't stop; keep going forward; let your soul live!'

Then we may realize that we have been created to head towards something infinite, something absolute. And we can make this discovery: it is sometimes in demanding situations that human beings become most fully themselves.

When we are supported by one another and do not let ourselves be brought to a halt by obstacles, when we know where to find the courage to keep going forward, then we realize that there is heartfelt joy, and even sheer happiness, in responding to God's call. Yes, God wants happiness for us!

And then something we never dared hope for appears. We leave behind the long nights with hardly a glimmer of light. Walking at times along ways of darkness, instead of weakening us, can even build us up within.

What means most to us is going from one discovery to another. Welcoming the coming day as God's today. Searching for peace of heart in all things. And life becomes beautiful ... yes, life will be beautiful.

Notes

1. See I John 4:10 and 19
2. See Luke 15:4–10
3. *Treatise on the Gospel of Luke*, V, 58
4. See Revelation 2:9
5. See Matthew 5:3–12
6. John 1:9
7. See John 1:1–2
8. See John 14:9
9. See John 14:16–20
10. Second Vatican Council, Pastoral Constitution *Gaudium et Spes* on the Church in the Modern World, no. 22, § 2
11. Encyclical *Redemptor Hominis*, no. 14
12. *Taizé, A Meaning to Life*, Chicago: GIA Publications, 1997, p. 62
13. *Quaestiones ad Thalassium*, XV
14. See John 14:16–20
15. See Matthew 28:20
16. See for example *Anna Karenina*, Penguin: London, 1978, p. 829ff
17. 2 Peter 1:19
18. John 21:17
19. 1 John 4:10 and 19

20. Saint Augustine, *Confessions*, I, 1
21. See 1 Thessalonians 5:19
22. Matthew 25:40
23. *The Shepherd of Hermas*, precept 42, 1 and 4
24. See 1 Timothy 2:4
25. Mark 10:21
26. Romans 8:26
27. See Luke 9:29 and Hebrews 5:7
28. See Luke 9:62
29. Saint Augustine, *Confessions*, XII, 10
30. See Philippians 4:6–7 and Ephesians 5:19
31. See Philippians 1:21–26
32. See John 3:17
33. See 1 Peter 2:23 and Luke 23:34
34. See Colossians 2:13
35. 1 John 3:20
36. 2 Peter 1:19
37. See Exodus 13:21–22
38. *Notes intimes*, Stock, 1984, p. 48
39. 2 Corinthians 12:10
40. *Journal of a Soul*, April/May 1930
41. See Galatians 2:20b
42. *Panorama* no. 340 (January 1999), p. 29
43. 1 John 4:8 and 16.
44. Quoted by Olivier Clément in *Taizé, A Meaning to Life*, p.77

45. See John 11:32–36
46. See John 17:26
47. See Matthew 28:20b
48. See Isaiah 53:2–4
49. See John 17:26 and Ephesians 1:3–5
50. See Matthew 18:20 and John 13:34–35
51. See John 17:20–23
52. Matthew 5:24
53. See Acts 4:32–35
54. *Service Orthodoxe de Presse* no. 244 (January 2000), p. 19
55. See Matthew 19:14
56. *The Sources of Taizé*, Continuum: London, 2000, p. 84
57. *Discourse to the Parish Priests of Rome*, February 1959
58. *Discourse at the Opening of the Council*, October 11, 1962
59. *Ibid.*
60. Olivier Clément, *Dialogues avec le Patriarche Athénagoras*, Fayard, 1969, p. 391
61. See John 1:4–5 and John 8:12
62. *Notebook.* 'Hosanna' is a Hebrew acclamation that expresses praise and thanksgiving to God.
63. *Letters*, vol. 1, letter no. 90 to Natalia Dmitrievna Fonvizina

64. See Psalm 42:3 and 5
65. See Matthew 28:20
66. See John 14:23
67. Matthew 7:7
68. John 17:26
69. Psalm 27:8
70. See John 15:13
71. *Commentary on the First Letter of Saint John,* 4, 6
72. Mark 9:24
73. See John 15:9
74. See Matthew 5,1–12 and Deuteronomy 4,40
75. Mark 5:36
76. Sirach 2:2
77. Matthew 25:40
78. 'God is Spirit' (John 4:24) and God's Spirit fills the entire universe (Wisdom 1:7)
79. 1 Peter 2:23–24
80. Romans 8:26
81. 1 Peter 2:21–25
82. John 15:11 and Luke 10:21
83. 'God's joy is your strength' (Nehemiah 8:10)
84. Genesis 2:7
85. See John 14:16–20

86. We already find this in the Gospel, where we see a man say to Christ, 'I believe.' But he immediately adds, 'Come and help my unbelief' (Mark 9:24).
87. John 14:1
88. See 1 Corinthians 13:2
89. See Baruch 5:1–9